BLOGGING MASTERCLASS PACKAGE 2018

MAHINROOP PM

PRINTED AND PUBLISHED

BY

AMAZON

Price

Ebook   : $3

Paperback: $6

Introduction

"Blogging Masterclass Package 2018" gives comprehensive and exact information about the art and science of blogging. An individual who is new to blogging will definitely benefit from the book "Blogging Masterclass Package 2018". This book has some excellent ideas on blogging and it serves as the perfect introductory guide to blogging. List of topics covered in the book include steps to successful blogging, best blogging platforms, making money with blogging, blog marketing plan, blogging tips, promoting the blog, effective blog writing styles and tips to launch a professional blog.

About the Author

MAHINROOP PM is an Information Technology Consultant based in India. He holds bachelors degree in Computer Science Engineering and masters degree in Business Administration. The author is passionate about technology, ecommerce, websites and books.

Written by MAHINROOP PM

This book is dedicated

To

Passionate bloggers all over the world

Table of Contents

Importance of Blogging

Have you ever thought that why blogging is absolutely important? Blogging is important due to innumerable reasons including the proper usage of free time, the opportunity to make money online, and gaining exposure.

Best blogging resources
Blogtyrant.com
Copyblogger.com
Problogger.net
Bloggingtips.com

Prospective bloggers should understand that blogging is not at all difficult and becoming a blogger is about learning how to blog. The blog of Freelancefolder.com will be of immense help to people passionate about making a killing on freelance writing business. The best feature of blog is that any computer literate can create blog and blogging software like the elegant WordPress has made blogging simplified. Blogging about our passion is definitely enriching and it will make us learn more about our passion. The task of blogging can be started to inspire youngsters who are facing challenges like starting a business, running an online business and advanced career opportunities. Blog can be used to do affiliate marketing and some bloggers sell digital products on their blog. Blogging portrays the blogger as an expert in his field and guest blogging will be helpful in gaining exposure. Another splendid benefit of blogging as a hobby is that it exposes our talent, creativity as well as passion.

Blogging is an excellent way to exhibit the talent of a prospective job seeker to an employer of his choice. If a blogger blogs consistently, it stands as a proof to his commitment, dedication, passion and creativity. Blogging improves the writing skills up to a great extent and communication skills can be improved by blogging. Blog is important in marketing and building relationship with customers and it is an effective marketing tool. Marketers use blogs to inform their customer base about new products and blogging creates better relationship among businesses and customers.

Major challenge in blogging is inadequate traffic and a blog will never ever flourish without targeted traffic. Just started out blogs need more exposure and quality content plays a major role in attracting visitors to a blog. In some cases, the niche of the blog may be the reason for insufficient web traffic to the blog. The blog should be optimized for search engines properly and effective search engine optimization techniques will pave the way towards increased traffic. Email list building is an essential part of blogging and the content in a blog should be interesting to the people irrespective of their age, gender and personal interests. Inclusion of amazing videos and eye catching pictures in a blog immediately grab visitor attention.

Distributing giveaways in blogging is an innovative idea and spelling and grammar mistakes in a blog should be avoided at all costs. A blog should be written keeping in mind the target audience and it shouldn't be written for search engines only. Driving targeted traffic to a blog is a continuous process and updating blog regularly is quite important. Unique and informative content in a blog or website will attract numerous visitors within a very short time span. Quality content creates indelible impressions about a typical blog of contemporary period driven by the explosive growth of internet.

High quality content is essential in retaining targeted traffic of a blog and advanced internet marketing techniques ensure that blogs get more exposure. Some of the most effective internet marketing techniques for blogs include social media marketing, search engine optimization, viral marketing, Pay per Click ads, and Google AdWords. Bloggers should use headlines that capture the attention of online audience and intelligent usage of infographics is recommended in a blog. Bloggers should pay special attention to engaging their audience, asking them questions, and replying to their comments. Experts should be invited to write content on our blog and the blog will get good reputation through guest blogging.

Selling high quality products will compel online audience to visit our blog and the product should be able to solve a particular problem. According to seasoned bloggers, a self hosted WordPress (WordPress.org) blog is the best option. Self hosted WordPress blog gives complete ownership as well as control on everything we do. Another commendable feature of WordPress is that it has tons of glaring themes and plug-ins. WordPress is completely free and it can be installed with few clicks within five or ten minutes.

Bloggers will have to spend few bucks on hosting and domain name and it will be worth the investment. Creating a distinctive brand forms the crux of blogging and brand is a well balanced combination of name, logo, visual element, and user experience. Each blog post should be well researched and it should have a clear as well as succinct point. It is often pointed out that bloggers should inject their personality into each and every blog post. The much publicized internet adage "Content is King" is applicable to blogging too and blogging on a regular basis is recommended for fruitful results. Visual content including videos, graphics, images and infographics has become a key ingredient of blogging.

Graphic design tools like the royal Canva can be used to create colourful visuals in blogging and connecting with other bloggers in the same niche is another essential blogging tip. Bloggers should pay attention to sharing other bloggers' content on social media platforms including Facebook and Twitter. Bloggers can use paid methods like Facebook advertising to get traffic to their blog and a blog of contemporary age should be responsive on mobile devices. Making a blog viewable on mobile devices has Search Engine Optimization benefits too and blog as well as plug-ins should be always up to date. Bloggers should ensure that they are running the latest versions of blog software and installation of WordPress security plug-in guards against online threats.

Most popular WordPress security plug-ins are WordFence, iThemes Security and Bullet Proof Security. Each blog post should be based around a basic keyword and that keyword should be included few times in a blog post. SEO plug-ins like Yoast SEO helps us to optimize blogs quickly and blogs often serve as an effective author platform. Blogging is considered as a creative outlet to express ideas, thoughts, opinions, beliefs and passions. It is often found that blogs have a great impact than social media posts and bloggers can gain large number of followers on social media channels through blogging.

Steps to Successful Blogging

Blogs will work effectively as a marketing tool if utilized properly and the blog topic should be an area which bloggers can enthusiastically write about. Keyword research tools like Google Zeitgeist and Yahoo Buzz Index help bloggers to find popular researched topics. It doesn't matter whether the blog topic is popular as long as it has large number of target audience. Updating the blog daily with multiple entries is recommended and there are numerous ways to build blog traffic including free advertising, RSS/XML feeds, and word of mouth. Blog URL should be used in the signature of email, message boards, chat forums and other communication media.

The blog post should be shared with family members, friends, colleagues and business partners. Many bloggers submit their blog content to article directories like GoArticles.com and ArticleCity.com. Free page counters like StatCounter.com (Real time web analytics service) can be used to track the blog traffic. An ideal web traffic service offers different services including advanced traffic analysis, keyword tracking information, visitors, returning visitors, and unique visitors. Multiple blog attracts different bloggers and bloggers should have blogs with Blogger.com, LiveJournal.com and tBlogs.com. Graphics give aesthetic beauty to a blog post and original graphics and arts are recommended in blogs.

Including personal experience in blog posts is a smart strategy and using the first person narrative is recommended. A theme like "Monday Investing Tip" or "Picture of the Week" attracts visitors to a particular blog. The payout in blogging is usually based on Pay per Click model and it is good to use graphical advertising including Amazon.com and BlogAds.com. There are numerous types of blogging software available including Squarespace.com and MovableType.org. Teaming up with one or more bloggers will help us to create a very powerful blog and the objective of teaming up in blogging is to make huge profits.

Blog is dedicated towards the distribution of news, opinion, commentary, and other content by individuals as well businesses alike. There are some bloggers who write for just the pleasure of writing and it is the culmination of writing excellence for them. Blog lets readers learn more about unique branding, value, products as well as services of a typical business. A successful blog is one that reaches a huge target audience, develops a following and builds credibility. A typical blogging niche should be something that enjoyed by the blogger and it will make blogging an easy experience. The success of the blog depends on the knowledge level of the blogger and the blogging niche should be based on knowledge and skill set.

Ability to write unique content distinguishes a successful blogger from another blogger and people who read blog are always in the lookout for fresh content. Writing unique content will help bloggers to learn more about branding and unique content sells like hot cakes. Bloggers should write to their readers as if they know each and every one of them personally and they should grab the attention of readers on the first paragraph of the blog post. Passionate bloggers who want to generate steady traffic to their blog should necessarily create a content schedule. Blog readers will notice consistency and the objective of a blogger should be to write one quality blog post per day.

Some well known blogs serve as online newspapers and readers will be interested to read fresh blog post while they sip morning coffee. Search engines including Google love blogs that deliver fresh content and these blogs made a lustrous win easily. The well known saying, "winners never quit and quitters never win" is applicable to blogging too. Innovative methods for blog marketing include viral marketing, social bookmarking, and advertising. The blog content shall be submitted to article directories for increased traffic and website traffic can be checked by tools such as Google Analytics.

To be persistent in blogging is absolutely important and a blogger should think from the user's perspective. An ideal blog should be creatively designed and it should have a logo, RSS (Really Simple Syndication) widget and social sharing buttons. Effective web marketing tips for blogging include announcing new blog through social networking websites, sharing blog with another blog and offering visitors to write on the blog. Blog serves as a high money spinning tool if utilized properly and keeping blog posts simple is extremely important. Over usage of graphics content in a blog is not recommended and keywords determine the success of blog ranking in search engines.

At least two keywords should appear in the blog domain name, blog title, and blog post content. Google Trends tool (Google's public web tool) should be used while blogging and affiliate marketers share links to their products, websites and personal email lists. Learning is the key to success in blogging and there are different ways of monetizing the blog including advertisements, affiliate marketing, selling products and selling advertisement space. Google AdSense is the most popular advertising method for blogs and affiliate marketers sell other people's products. Some innovative bloggers equipped with effulgence of creativity sell information products like books, eBooks, video tutorial, audio program and CDs through their blogs.

The number one task is to start blogging with our own blog and a blogging niche is subset of market or target market. It is often pointed out that majority of the blogs use domain names that are short and easy to remember. A good domain name should be optimized to suit the keywords for blog and higher search engine ranking leads to higher traffic potential for blog. Original content will improve search engine ranking and it is to be kept in mind that successful blogging is an art and science. Blogging is a simple way to get started our star studded career as an internet marketer and successful blogging is a game of quality content.

One of the most important characteristics of a blog is credibility and successful blogging is a give and take task. Reading blogs in the same niche would often be helpful and forum posting and guest posting can be effectively used to market a blog. Keyword research is considered as the most important step to build a successful blog and a blog should be planned just like planning a traditional business. A prospective blogger should ask himself the below given questions.

Why do I want to start a blog?

What services can I render?

Are people looking for the same service?

How wide is the market?

Best Blogging Platforms

I have compiled the list of best blogging platforms and it includes WordPress, Weebly, Blogger, Tumblr, and Squarespace.

WordPress

WordPress.com is for bloggers looking for free blogging sites where as WordPress.org demands hosting by the user. Bloggers will have to spend few bucks to get WordPress hosting and WordPress has streamlined innovation in content management system. WordPress.org is an open source website builder and it is known among bloggers all over the world for flexibility. Thousands of mesmerizing themes are available for WordPress and the availability of free plug-ins is another top rated feature of WordPress. WordPress.org is one of the best blogging platforms for ecommerce and WordPress.com is a software service company which offers hosting services.

WordPress.com is not customizable and bloggers will have to pay for removal of third party advertisements in WordPress.com. WordPress powers millions of websites all over the world including CNN, PlayStation, New York Times blogs and Ford. Website designers, website developers and users rate WordPress as an effective content management system with stellar reputation. Business sites, job boards, and classified advertisement sites make use of WordPress and the free availability of WordPress makes it a Content Management System with a difference. Search engines including Google have fallen in love with WordPress since it uses well written code.

Weebly

Weebly is another popular blogging platform and easy drag and drop feature is the most talked about feature of Weebly. Persons with no technical knowledge can use Weebly every easily and attractive design and layout choice punctuate Weebly. Bloggers looking to build small or simple websites or blogs can use Weebly and get amazing results. Weebly depicts the grace of blossoming blogging landscape and free hosting service is the eloquent attraction of Weebly. This splendid blog software has a platform built for ecommerce and Weebly offers infinite options for monetizing including Google AdSense, banner advertisements and third party codes.

Time Magazine has selected Weebly as one of the best 50 websites of 2007 and it has more than five billion registered users. User friendly and intuitive website designing platform helps Weebly to stand out from their competitors. Weebly has a paid version too and the free version of Weebly is more than enough for a blogging enthusiast. Free Weebly website can be populated with pictures, galleries, contact forms, slideshows, YouTube videos and Google maps. Weebly offers a platform to sell products and PayPal can be integrated with Weebly very quickly. Basic elements of Weebly are content elements, two column layouts, custom HTML and contact capture forms.

Blogger

Exclusive free hosting is the elegant attraction of Blogger and this free blogging software is highly recommended for beginners. Blogger is one of the largest blogging sites on the internet today and it allows creating a private discussion group. Easiness, easy to change themes and fully functional dashboard make Blogger highly popular among the blogger community. There is no need to install anything in blogger and people coming from non technical platform can utilize Blogger. Making money with Google AdSense is something more than getting traffic to the blog and Blogger.com is owned by Google.

The blog name used in Blogger.com should be easy to remember and the new version of blogger allows hosting domain at Google server at dns.google.com. Blogger is known as a powerful blog software and drag and drop features in Blogger are easy to work with. Both starters and professional bloggers make use of Blogger.com and Blogger blogs are ranked well in Google search engine. Commendable features of Blogger include RSS feed, video, newsreel, slideshow, countdown widget as well as polls. Blogger allows users to change colours of the templates, edit the HTML (Hypertext Markup Language) and CSS (Cascading Style Sheets). Custom HTML box in Blogger allows putting advertisements from affiliate programs of EBay and Amazon.

Tumblr

Tumblr is undoubtedly one of the best blogging platforms available today and simplicity to use is the fabled attraction of Tumblr. It has unique similarities with social networking sites and it is a community based website with likeable image gallery. High quality premium themes of Tumblr are available at affordable price tags and it has a fantastic mobile application. Tumblr can be converted into a custom website and it is a massive social platform with impeccable records. The impressive list of Tumblr customers include world famous bands and musicians known for their electrifying performance.

Tumblr has rocketed into prominence as a personal creative blogging space and social networking folks rate Tumblr as an excellent platform. It is a blogging platform recommended for ecommerce and Tumblr has emerged successful in combining blogging and social media. Tumblr is a great source of content equipped with user interaction and creating content in Tumblr is super easy. It can be aptly referred as a blog merged with social media and Tumblr is great for Search Engine Optimization purposes. Tumblr lets users to connect to Google Analytics account and it is home to numerous niche blogs available today. Users can share images, video, music or any kind of multimedia in Tumblr very quickly as well as easily.

Squarespace

Squarespace is highly functional free blogging software and user friendliness acts as the halo of success of Squarespace. It offers a splendid collection of themes and full time support is another feature of Squarespace, a plausible blogging initiative. The plans of Squarespace start from $8 and it allows us to add twenty pages, one blog and two contributors. Ease of use is the number one plus point of Squarespace and it lets us to create fully functional site with clean design. Nice collections of widgets are another super attraction of Squarespace and drop down menus, drag and drop functionality and built in tutorial makes Squarespace the favourite of bloggers.

Easy comment management and excellent technical support are the best features of Squarespace software. Feature rich services of Squarespace made it highly popular among the blogging community. Squarespace loads quickly since they are not flash based sites and mobile visitors will be able to experience the functionality of a website without losing its charm in Squarespace. It has launched an app which gives users control over their site or blog using iPhone and it features one touch synchronization capability with desktop computer. Squarespace is a unique blog importing tool and the customization of site is virtually unlimited in Squarespace.

Making Money with Blogging

Context advertisements, selling advertising space, affiliate marketing, CPA (Cost per Action), selling products and services are the most prominent methods for money making with blogging. Bloggers sign up for advertising sites like Chitika and Google AdSense to add advertising links to their blog. Google gives a percentage of revenue to the blogger whenever a reader clicks on the link or view advertisements. Advertising space on blog can be offered to companies for a monthly price and selling advertisement space guarantees monthly income. Blog enthusiasts can make money by writing blog posts for fellow bloggers or promoting products on their own blog.

Some blog sites pay a flat fee for writing specific advertisement and sites like Blogsvertise and Pay per Post offer these services. Affiliate marketing is a performance type marketing in which a business rewards affiliates for each product bought through the affiliate's marketing efforts. Chitika Mini Malls and Amazon Associates are the two affiliate marketing programs preferred by bloggers. Email list on affiliate marketing platforms lets visitors sign on to a newsletter or free offering that prompts them to give their email address. Bloggers get paid for completing a task for companies and advertisers in Cost per Action (CPA). Bloggers offer the services of writing, website designing and photo editing through their blog and the blog can be converted into an Ebook.

Companies like Apple, Amazon and Smashwords allow bloggers to self publish their Ebooks and the Ebook platform of Amazon is known as Kindle Direct Publishing. Many bloggers have successfully tested the method of getting donations to their blog and payment gateways like PayPal and Payza let bloggers to accept donations. Regular maintenance of the blog is recommended and blogs can be promoted through social media channels too. Bloggers can start blogging consulting through their blogs and website flipping is another unique strategy to make money with blogs. The widgets and templates of WordPress blog come as Google AdSense ready and the amount of money made in AdSense depends on many factors including how many visitors come to the blog and the type of advertisements showing up on the blog.

Bloggers can sell other people's products through blogs and earn money as an affiliate in sites like Click Bank. Joining Google AdSense is absolutely free and the blogs serve as a medium between readers and online store in affiliate programs. Reviewing niche products is another smart strategy of making money online with blogging and it is almost similar to affiliate marketing. Focusing on blog topic on what most people don't take seriously and focusing on a niche that is not saturated are two essential blogging money making tips.

Making money with blogging will definitely take some time and bloggers who make a killing on blogging make use of video casting and podcasting in their blogs. The blogging phrase targeted should have low competition, but high search volume and getting quality back links from credible sources is smart blogging money making tip. Starting a blog identical to the subject of affiliate marketing program is recommended and blog advertising becomes more profitable when it is turned into blog partnership. Some blog partners pay bloggers a "per post" rate and blogging is an appealing way to make money online. Bloggers should host their blog instead of free hosting and search engine optimization, blog commenting, and forum marketing pave the way towards increased number of visitors to the blog site.

Bloggers should not use highly technical words in blogging if their objective is to make money with blogging. Digital products, software and information products can be sold through blogs and it is an excellent way of blog monetization. Google AdSense has helped thousands of bloggers to make tons of money and Google delivers the relevant text and image for blogger's website. The referral feature of Google AdSense helps bloggers to generate additional income by displaying Google's referral button on the web page.

Bloggers can start with Google AdSense by completing an online application at https://www.google.com/adsense/start/. Passionate bloggers will have to copy and paste HTML code provided by Google to their web page and they will have to comply with Google's program policies. It doesn't cost anything if we have a website to join Google AdSense and Google AdSense is a classic way to make money from home. Google will pay bloggers monthly if their earning is above $100 and the AdSense program is not restricted to high page rank sites. Google approves the websites within two to three days and Google ads placed above the fold will perform better.

Google AdSense can be used to make money from mobile content, video content and website content. The search engine giant Google uses an auction based system that allows advertisers to compete for top bids. Bloggers can make about 68% from displaying Google AdWords on the site and good quality content is the most important thing as far as making money from Google AdSense is concerned. Google locates relevant advertisements by finding the keywords on web pages and our website will get more clicks using the AdSense. Content relevancy is important to the success of Google AdSense and anybody who wants to place advertisements on their sites using Google AdSense gets paid by Google.

There will be a Google Analytics account associated with AdSense which provides web statistics and the entire process of making money with blogging through AdSense is simple. If a user has an existing Google account, he can apply for a Google AdSense account under the same account. Bloggers should test advertisement by different colours of the text, headings, URL and the placement of ads on the website. Three essential steps of Google AdSense are targeting websites to specific niches, matching the colour of AdSense ads to the colour of the website and driving lots of high quality targeted traffic. Google AdSense provides immediate positive results and it is the top rated attraction of the one and only Google AdSense.

Google AdSense gives bloggers the opportunity to customize links, borders and colour themes of the advertisement. The AdSense channel will let us know how well the advertisements or links are doing and Google AdSense has gained riveting achievement as a Pay per Click program. Putting AdSense advertisements on many websites will help us to gain more money and Google allows maximum three ad units. AdSense can be integrated to articles published in HubPages (User generated content sharing website). Websites generating at least hundred visits per day from search engines will create some amount of passive income.

Blog Marketing Plan

Social media is a great business tool for blog marketing and people on Facebook, Google Plus, and LinkedIn may be interested in our blogs. Bloggers should notify social media networks about their new blog posts and bookmarking is another prominent blog marketing method. There are lots of sites where members keep bookmarks of blogs that they want to read later and it will give the writer great exposure. Onlywire.com is a prominent automated bookmarking service used for the purpose of blog marketing. Article directories like Ezine articles and Go Articles can be used for effective blog marketing and articles from these directories show up in search engine results.

Article marketing is a way to get our blog out there and show people what we have to offer (Sites like Ezine articles require bio). Bloggers should create a presence on social media sites including the marvellous Facebook and Twitter. Videos and podcasts are other top notch tools for blog marketing of contemporary age and videos should be distributed to video directories including YouTube. There are other fantastic video directories available for blog marketing including Daily Motion and Meta Café. Podcasting is a smart blog marketing plan and podcast refers to an internet radio program where we are the guest or host.

The uploaded podcast on our site will be automatically distributed to iTunes (media player and media library). Blog commenting forms an important part of blog marketing and bloggers should ensure that they respond to relevant comments. Interviewing an expert and publishing it on the blog is an attractive blog marketing strategy. Submitting press releases is another effective way to market the blog and creating a press release is within the budget of companies. Posting on blog about current affairs is another blog promotion strategy and a well marketed blog will be a great asset to any business organization.

The content in a typical blog should be search engine optimized and link exchanges are wonderful for blog marketing. Paid directories are another blog marketing tool and it allows bloggers to list blog in their directory under specific category. We will get more readers if we get more links to our blogs and RSS feed gives website owners permission to publish blogs on their website. Another way to exchange links is to find sites which are related to the product we are promoting and asking them for link exchange. Blog marketing is a great strategy to sell products and promote affiliate programs using the links.

Contests are another way to market a blog and it will keep readers coming back to the blog again and again. Blog address can be added to email signature line and consistency is very important as far as blog marketing efforts are concerned. If the typical blog is about aquarium keeping, bloggers can include interview with a successful aquarium keeping hobbyist in their blog. Current events in our market create great blog posts and proper keyword density should be maintained in every blog post. Back links can be generated through article commenting, article writing, as well as social bookmarking.

Guest blogging increases visibility to new bloggers and it leads to a business connection with bloggers in the same niche. Establishing a niche, establishing primary keywords for the niche, constant blog posts, submit feeds to feed directories, commenting on other blogs within the niche market, developing back links and generating new readership through guest blogging are the steps involved in blog marketing. Blog marketing is the perfect way to attract more customers and making blog important to readers forms the crux of blog marketing. The blog should get indexed in the search engines for better visibility and generating links for blogs will be beneficial in blogging.

Blog marketing includes marketing through advertisements placed on the blogs, recommendations by the blogger, and cross syndication of content in different blogs. Blog advertisements are often found in the form of banners, text links, flash animation, streaming video and audio clips. Owners of blogs monetize their blogs through a combination of advertisement networks including the Google AdSense. The greatest blog marketing strategy is definitely the viral marketing and it can be done at very little cost to the advertiser. Blog marketing gives a great opportunity for marketing agencies, businesses and public relations professionals.

Blog marketing is inexpensive to start off with and WordPress.org is the recommended self hosted option for blogs. Offering tips, updates and fresh content attracts visitors to come back to a blog again and again. Many entrepreneurs use blogging for search engine optimization and blog marketing acts as an emblazonry to online businesses. Blogs help bloggers to establish their expertise and credibility in a particular niche such as business, personal finance, real estate, and investing. Blogs allow businesses to have a conversation with their market and building trust with customers is the hallmark of blog marketing. Blog marketing has great revenue earning potential consisting of advertising, affiliate marketing and sponsorship.

Businesses should use the same logo in their blogs and website and free blog platform is not recommended for business blogging. Blog should be included in all the marketing materials of a business organization and blogs can be used to encourage email signups. The blog system has become a reliable business model for bloggers based in the United States of America. Companies, online stores and big brands have recognized the power of blog marketing and they are pursuing all possible avenues to get the maximum benefit from blogging. The objectives should be clearly defined before choosing a blog marketing plan and blog marketing is suitable for the launch of a new product and branding.

Brand awareness can be strengthened through blog marketing and it provides a platform to launch products in the market as a part of testing. High flexibility and speed are the commendable features of blog marketing and effective blog marketing strategies will make a blog an instant hit. An ideal blog works perfectly as a content marketing hub and blogs fuel social media and sales. Blogs act as owned media, social media, search engine optimization tool, sales vehicle, and streamlined Content Management System. A blog is a marketing channel to get our message out on a 24/7 basis and blogs provide the basis of building a targeted community.

Blogging Tips

Bloggers should adopt an educator's mentality and they can gain reader's trust very easily and feedbacks should be encouraged in blogging. A prominent blogging tip is to use images, infographics, illustrations and charts in respective blogs. Bloggers should be consistent in blogging and using keyword phrases that increase search engine ranking is absolutely important. SEO (Search Engine Optimization) plug-ins should be installed in a blog and successful bloggers are master storytellers. Real customers and real solutions should be cited in a blog post and bloggers should invest in hiring the best writers and designers.

A call to action should be included in a blog post and the old saying "Practice makes perfect" is applicable to blogging too. Another essential blogging tip is to update the blog daily and an ideal blogging platform should be affordable and easy to use. Bloggers should take advantage of web 2.0 marketing and they should have a crystal clear idea about how to drive traffic to their site. A blog can be search engine optimized using the SEO plug-in SEOPressor and the blog name should contain keywords. The domain name of a blog should be easy to spell and bloggers can exchange links with other blogs in the same niche.

Finding popular keyword related to blog posts is an absolute must and 2-3 keywords should be used in blog title. The keyword should be used in the domain name, blog title, hyper link, ALT tag, and title tag of a blog. Post title optimization widget should be used in a blog and "All-in-one-SEO" is a great tool for Meta tag and title optimization. The layout of the blog should be beautiful and a nicely designed blog layout is an elegant attraction. Content quality is the most important thing that determines the success and monetization of a blog.

Blog visitor should be able to find recent posts and labels very easily and image optimization should be done in a blog post for better visibility. Loading time of the blog should not be too long and bloggers should ensure that widgets installed by them don't slow down the loading. JPEG and PNG files should be used in blog posts and Photoshop is the recommended image editing software for blogging. Every blog post should be written after conducting proper research and it is a great idea to include sub titles. The blog should be written in simple English and bloggers should give links to useful resources of their topics.

Giving resources related to blog topic improves internal linking of the blog and bloggers should encourage readers to interact and comment. An ideal blog should use professional looking theme, template as well as header image and it is best to use 3 column template with 1024/768 resolution. The font colour and size should be designed in such a manner that permits readers to view the blog in different screen resolutions. The blog visibility should be checked in different web browsers including Mozilla Firefox, Google Chrome, Apple Safari and Opera. Google AdSense advertisements in a blog post should be used in post body and right hand side bar.

There should not be too many outgoing links in a typical blog post and "All in One SEO" plug-in can be used to create Meta tag for individual posts. A blog should be based on the real passion of a blogger and bloggers should consider the suggestions of readers. Freshness of the blog content enchants readers and bloggers should keep in mind that blogging is not a get rich quick scheme. A tool like Google AdWords can be used for blog keyword research and it will tell us how many people are searching for a particular keyword on a monthly basis.

The keyword density (Percentage of times a keyword appears on a web page) in a blog post should be maintained between 1-2 percent. Keyword should be used in the first and last sentences of a blog post and three different header tags of H1, H2 and H3 should be used in a blog. According to well experienced bloggers, the keyword in a typical blog post should be bolded, underlined and italicized. Adding video to a blog is a splendid tip and bloggers need video camera, iPhone and webcam to get started. A blog post should be ideally of 500-700 words and proper usage of images in blog is once again reiterated.

Bloggers should understand that "a picture is a thousand words" and tags should be used in a blog post since they tell readers quickly what the blog post is about. It is recommended to create a Facebook page for blogs and Twitter is another prominent blog marketing tool. The PDF version of blog post can be submitted to document sharing websites including Box and SlideShare. One of the easiest blogging tips is to set up an email subscription and online blogging is about giving incentives to people opting for email list.

Another key blogging technique is to submit the blog to prominent blog directories and understanding target audience forms the basis of blogging. Email marketing can be used to monetize a blog and writing in-depth articles is important since Google ranks 2000+ word articles well. Bloggers should write two in-depth 2000 word articles instead of ten short articles in their blog. Building quality links and increasing the overall domain authority is another vital blogging tip of today. Well researched and well written quality content will pave the way towards increased organic traffic.

Getting testimonials from experts is another blogging tip. If readers share quality blog content on social media channels, it will attract back links from other blogs naturally. Bloggers should keep in mind that Search Engine Optimization is all about quality back links and keyword research. There are lots of ways to increase traffic to blog including social media, email list, videos, content marketing and blog commenting. Blog should be monetized right from the first day of blogging and creation of the email list should be started before the blog launch. It is to be pointed out that giveaways boost email subscription rates and ebook or video course can be distributed as a giveaway.

Web Hosting Tips for Blogging

Web hosting is a type of internet hosting service and web hosting companies provide space in servers owned by them. It gives users the chance to upload a specific file by making use of File Transfer Protocol and blogging web hosting plans are often inexpensive. Bloggers should select WordPress hosting for secure web hosting and advanced protection is the hallmark of WordPress web hosting. Numerous high traffic sites utilize WordPress web hosting platform and server security is an important requirement for web hosting. WordPress hosting offers protected and virtualized servers and it protects the website from attempts of hacking.

Reseller hosting is a type of hosting in which the account holder uses his granted space to host sites by third party. It is cheaper than other types of hosting and bloggers should have a basic understanding of the technical features of web hosting. Bloggers of huge websites can consider upgrading to dedicated servers and the hosting company should be put on trial first. Monthly contract with web hosting provider is recommended for bloggers and free hosting is not a recommended option for making money with blogging. Web hosting package for blogs start from a minimum of $5 per month and signing up for a one year contract is often found as the best option.

Paid hosting allows bloggers to have full control on their domain name and bandwidth, disk space, traffic and database are other recommended features of paid hosting. Web hosting package allows bloggers to have control over the front end and back end of their website. The features of top rated web hosting providers are unlimited disk space, unlimited bandwidth, free site builder with templates, control panel, money back guarantee, and 99.9% up time guarantee. HostGator is a reliable provider of web hosting services and many hosting companies choose tools as a part of their account. The best web hosting for WordPress will exceed WordPress minimum requirement and it will have the latest versions of Apache, MySQL and PHP.

Thousands of free upgrades and enhancements is another striking attraction of WordPress as a web hosting tool. HostGator is the favourite hosting plan of internet marketers and bloggers and they have awesome customer support. They stay current on the latest WordPress changes and Site5 is another well known hosting provider for blogging. The cloud hosting offered by Site5 can increase site ranking with better load speed and millions of websites are hosted by Host Gator. Site5 is known among bloggers as a reliable and affordable web hosting service provider and they are proponents of intuitive web hosting.

Choosing a reliable web hosting provider is essential for the success of blog and a blog with good amount of traffic needs greater bandwidth. DreamHost, Laughing Squid and Blue Host are the well known website hosting providers in the world. Reasonable price is the first and foremost quality of a web hosting company and it is recommended to check prices of different web hosting companies. Prominent web hosting services are equipped with user friendly control panel and there would be multiple ways to contact a hosting company including email, ticket system and phone. Many web hosting companies provide yearly subscription rates and the control panel should allow us to install WordPress within few clicks.

Some web hosting companies provide the option to upgrade to Virtual Private Server or dedicated server. Bloggers should select web hosting companies providing email hosting and email within domain name sounds more professional. Blogging enthusiasts who want to upload videos, infographics and photos should select web hosting companies providing high storage solutions. The deciding factors of web hosting for blogs are given below.

Do we need server root access?

Do we need automatic backup?

Do we need automated malware scanning?

Can we tweak and secure the WordPress ourselves?

NameCheap and GoDaddy are the favourites of bloggers for registering a domain name and the site uptime can be checked using tools like Uptime Robot. Backing up blog regularly is important and shared hosting, VPS (Virtual Private Server) hosting, dedicated hosting and cloud hosting are the different types of web hosting. Affordability and ease of use are the principal advantages of shared hosting whereas the elegant attractions of VPS hosting are root server access and secured environment. Maximum control and great server performance are the top rated attractions of dedicated hosting. Server scalability and cost efficiency are the most talked about features of cloud hosting and it is ideal to select a web host that we can afford for at least two years.

Bloggers should monitor blog memory usage on a regular basis and they should consider upgrading to VPS hosting once the blog hits eight percent of the allocated memory. SSD (Solid State Drive) hosting can be used for better site speed and it is recommended to choose a .com domain. According to web hosting providers, .com domains are established, credible, and memorable. Most smartphone keyboards have an automatic .com button and the domain name should be kept under 15 characters. Free and self hosted WordPress blogs will serve the real purpose of getting the messages out and increasing traffic to websites.

WordPress allows users to switch between code view and WYSIWYG (What You See is What You Get) editor. Web hosting allows the usage of advanced languages like PHP (Hypertext Preprocessor), ASP (Active Server Pages), Perl and Python. The shared hosting web hosting plan offers sharing the resources of a single server with other customers. The technical support of a web hosting company should be available on a 24/7 basis and shared hosting is the cheapest type of web hosting. Dedicated hosting is the most expensive and sophisticated type of web hosting available today.

Reading the online reviews of web hosting companies will help us to make an informed decision about the web hosting provider. CPanel in a web host allows to easily add applications to the site and it is useful for setting up email, database administration, file management, FTP and installation of scripts. The cPanel comes along with Fantastico, an installer for the WordPress blog platform and forums. Some web hosting companies provide multiple domain hosting and unlimited email account is a great feature provided by majority of the web hosting companies. There should be backup for files, databases, and server settings in the web hosting package offered by a provider. Quality, reliability and feature richness are the splendid attractions of an ideal web hosting plan.

Promoting the Blog

Self hosted WordPress blog is an industry standard for their ease of use, flexibility and feature richness. A blog should have necessary plug-ins before the blog launch strategy and blog promotion strategies ensure that bloggers get exposure, traffic, opt-ins, shares and search engine rankings.

Initial Blog Promotion Strategy

Ping list is a list of websites that listen for new content on the web and WordPress provides a comprehensive list of ping services. Feed burner offers a way for users to subscribe new blog content and users will be notified whenever new content gets published. WordPress SEO by Yoast and SEO Pressor are the top rated Search Engine Optimization plug-ins. Functionality and automation are the best features of Search Engine Optimization plug-ins made for blogs. They take care of on page SEO and there are both free and paid directories available for blogs. Social bookmarking brings traffic to a site and bloggers should bookmark articles from variety of sources. Most popular social bookmarking sites are Stumble Upon, Digg, Reddit, Delicious, and Diigo. Bloggers should make use of social bookmarking automation tools and they can get repeated traffic to their site by sending email subscribers blog broadcast. According to internet marketing experts, Get Response and Aweber are the recommended auto responder services for blogging.

Both Get Response and Aweber are almost equivalent in their features and the opt-in form of auto responder service will capture the subscriber's email address. The giveaway of auto responder will be MP3 audio, video tutorial, ebook, online course, and cheat sheet. Blog broadcast is an automated email that can be sent to subscriber list containing content of the blog post. Maximizing the built in RSS features of the blog is recommended and bloggers can add additional functionality to the RSS feed at the Feed Burner website. Promoting the blog is the hardest part of the business and credibility promotes the blog up to a great extent.

Bloggers should ensure that their blog is included in the business card and it should be placed at the local bulletin boards of restaurants. Flyers and stickers are two elegant offline blog promotion methods and it is an innovative idea to submit blog posts to local newspapers. Bloggers can introduce their blogs to friends, family members, customers, and business partners with an email that gives information on what the blog is about. Sites like MyBlogLog, Blog

Catalog, and Networked Blogs can be used to promote and market a blog. Facebook and LinkedIn can be effectively used to reach more blog readers and bloggers should provide value to readers by building relationships.

Micro blogging sites like Twitter can be used to promote blogs irrespective of their genre and blog promotion is an integral part of the overall advertising strategy. According to bloggers who emerged victorious in blogging, blogs can be promoted by creating new content and receiving quality back links. The key focus of blog promotion strategy is to build as many inbound links as possible and the blog will start to rank well in search engines. More bloggers of today venture into the blog content syndication and the concept behind blog content syndication is getting content to as much blog posts as possible. Blog content syndication will attract targeted traffic to the blog and on page optimization of blogs include keyword analysis, Meta tag generation, content optimization, sitemap, and W3C validation.

Most of the blog promotion methods can be automated and social media optimization helps to raise awareness of the blog. Bloggers can share URL containing news, business offers and discounts on social media channels. Text link advertising will bring lots of traffic to the blog and press release is an efficient way to get traffic to a blog. Press releases about the blog can be mailed to the editors of newspapers, magazines, radio stations, and television networks.

Facebook is definitely an amazing platform for blog promotion and Facebook fan page will allow us to promote a free gift with an opt-in box. A Facebook page permits bloggers to email their fans few times a week and the fans can be kept up to date on recent promotions. Guest blogging is a technique used by bloggers by writing articles on someone else's blog site. It is popular among bloggers for its capacity of building web traffic and quality back links. The guest blogging article written by a blogger should be authoritative and informative and its objective is to create a positive impression about the blog.

Some blog directories are open to specific niche blogs and bloggers who are active in at least one social network tend to bring more traffic. It is to be kept in mind that blog promotion takes time, effort, perseverance as well as hard work. Bloggers can charge businesses to post links on their blog and another blog promotion option is to periodically send online friends private messages about our blog. Article commenting is another well known blog promotion strategy and big article directories feature article commenting. YouTube commenting is a blog promotion strategy which will bring huge traffic to the blog.

The blog posts written in Google Docs can be made public and putting a link back to the blog is recommended. Blog posts can be converted into free ebooks and a free offer should be given inside the ebook. Blog carnival is a great way to promote the blog for free and bloggers can include affiliate links or links to their own products in blogs. Yahoo! Answers is an excellent way to drive targeted traffic and building email list is the most effective blog promotion strategy. Email list is the best way to get organic traffic to the website and some excellent tools for email list building are SumoMe plug-in and List Builder.

It seems that OptinMonster and Lead Pages are the most popular tools for email list building.

<u>Steps in Email List Building</u>

Weekdays work best for promoting blogs through email and email listing amplifies social sharing from our loyal audience. Bloggers should send plain text emails to their subscribers to keep it personal and seasoned bloggers recommend starting an email newsletter. A marketing automation tool like Active Campaign can be used in blogging and "Share Link Generator" is used to write social messages and drop it in the link to blog post.

<u>Tips to Maximize New Blog Post Email</u>

Guest Blogging

Guest blogging is a highly recommended blog promotion strategy and the benefits of guest blogging will become tangible in the coming weeks, months and years. It exposes the blog to a huge audience and guest blogging is the process of creating content and publishing it on another blog in the same niche. Guest blogger gives out his content for free and they will benefit from guest blogging via targeted traffic. Guest bloggers should write only in blogs with better search engine rankings and finding blogs belonging to the same niche is the first step of guest blogging.

The bio in a guest blog should include areas of knowledge, description of the blog and a link to it.

Graphics, charts and images should be used in a guest blog post in order to make it appealing. Pursuing guest blogging will enable bloggers to become thought leaders in their industry.

Advantages of Guest Blogging

If a blogger has few guest posts on a topic, people will consider him as an expert in the particular niche. Bloggers are allowed to add a link to their blog in guest post and it will help to create invaluable back links. It is important that bloggers should be consistent in their guest blogging efforts and guest blogs should be to the point and precise.

The guest blog post write up should be equipped with informative content, proper formatting, and polite tone. Getting quality back links is a standard Search Engine Optimization technique and guest blogging improves the writing skills of a blogger. Guest blogging helps to build a popular social media profile and the guest blog post can be broken up into headings, images and bullet points. It helps to build relationship with other bloggers in the same niche and guest blogging is an essential component of branding. Google and other prominent search engines like related links inside the blog post and having guest posts on a lot of blogs related to the topic is important.

Guest blogging is a great alternative to article marketing and the most important tips for guest blogging are choosing the right blogs, establishing a beneficial agreement and coming up with the right blog content. The goal of a guest blogger is to find new readers for his blog and bloggers can write guest blog posts on new blogs with a loyal following. Guest blogging is a win-win situation for both the guest blogger and the host blogger and the guest blogger gets exposure to new audience and boost in web traffic.

Guest blog posts should be written from the perspective of target audience and guest blogging helps to get targeted stream of web traffic. Guest bloggers need to build traffic in order to get popularity and income and the link placed in the guest blog post will be seen by the search engines. Many guest blogs allow additional blogger information such as photo, biography and social media links. Images used in a blog post should be our own or royalty free images and incentivizing guest bloggers is a fantastic idea. Guest blogging is usually free of charge for the guest blogger and host blogger and guest bloggers can position themselves as an authority with the right content guest blog posts.

The guest blog should have engaged readership and Google is a great place to find the best guest blogging opportunities. Guest bloggers should use the keywords of "Submit a guest post"," guest post", "guest post by" and "guest post guidelines" in Google search. The quality of guest blog posts is determined by the below given criteria.

Does our subject matter expertise showed in our guest post?

Is our writing free of grammatical errors and spelling mistakes?

Does our writing include reliable sources?

Do guest posts receive likes, shares or comments?

The agreement between the guest blogger and the host blogger should specify word count of the post and publication date.

List of Guest Blogging Sites

1. Kissmetrics
2. Traffic Generation Cafe
3. Firepole Marketing
4. Mashable
5. MarketingProfs
6. Men with Pens
7. Social Media Examiner
8. Moss
9. Smart Passive Income
10. DIY Themes
11. She Takes on the World
12. Inspiration Feed
13. Birds on the Blog
14. Social Fresh
15. The ReadHead Writing Blog
16. Blog Godown
17. Bloggers Passion
18. ComLuv
19. Famous Bloggers
20. We Blog Better

Bloggers should consider featuring blog posts written by guest bloggers and research is an essential component of guest blogging. Blogging aficionados should ask the below given questions themselves before featuring guest blogger's blog posts.

Do they have a list of active followers who post comments and shares?

Do they have a Facebook page or Twitter profile where they share blog posts?

A guest blog should be treated as a valuable piece of information and the ultimate objective of a guest blog is to educate the reader. According to the opinion of smart bloggers, the author bio and tagline in a guest blog post should be clear as well as concise. Each guest blog post should be concluded with a call to action and bloggers can use Google Analytics to track how much traffic the guest post generates.

Guest blogging is a great way to increase site rank in Google searches and guest bloggers make up a big portion of conversations going on the internet. The best feature of guest blogging is that it allows us to enter an already established community and the rules of being a good guest blogger are outlined below.

Link to the post from our blog

Promote the blog post on Twitter

Share it on Facebook

Send a "Thank You" message to the blogger

Reply to comments on the post

According to internet marketing luminaries, guest posting on other sites is five times as valuable as creating new content on our site. Guest posting is undoubtedly an excellent method for extending reach and boosting the reputation online. It is a fantastic way to get our write ups featured in news sites, magazines and newspapers and become a rock star blogger. Guest blogging is one of the best marketing strategies available today and the benefits of guest blogging are instant exposure to targeted traffic, expanding personal network, growing social media following and improving online authority. Bloggers can optimize their landing pages, CTAs (Click through Rate) and other elements to boost their conversion rates.

Ways to Drive Traffic to Blog

Traffic is absolutely important to the success of any blog and the goals should be clearly set before driving traffic to the blog. Writing quality blog posts is the first tip to driving traffic to the blog and an ideal bog post should be well researched. Free back links and personal branding are the benefits of blog commenting and bloggers should comment only when they can add some value. It is important to get high quality back links for good Moz ranking and the blog should be optimized for search engines. Bloggers should have a basic understanding of on page SEO factors and they should participate in forums related to the niche.

Writing list posts is another great idea to drive traffic to the website and bloggers can write about how to drive traffic to their blog too. Innovative bloggers write for tutorial sites like Tutorialized.com and they can work on getting their blog covered by media. Top bloggers join in blog communities like MMO Social Network and Blog Engage and the blog can be pinged using a site like Pingomatic. Starting a giveaway or blog contest is another well known idea to drive traffic to the website. Bloggers can create videos about their niche and distribute it to video sites using services like Tubemogul.com.

Blog URL can be used as signature in our email and bloggers can submit blogs to blog directories which will distribute post to many sites. It is a good practice to write a press release about the blog post and submit it to free press release submission sites. The blog can be advertised using Facebook Ads and super smart bloggers advertise their blogs on local television station, local radio station and newspaper. Blogs can be advertised on online yellow pages and it is recommended to create professional Twitter account, get some followers and start tweeting the blog posts. Social sharing buttons enable bloggers to gain more traffic when people share the blog post and bloggers should ensure that they use tags in their blog post.

Blogging fans can answer questions on Yahoo! Answers and use their blog as a source of traffic. Creative bloggers write a blog post featuring top influencers in their niche and a classic example is top ten internet marketing blogs. Bloggers who have made a tremendous achievement in blogging interview top bloggers in their niche and publish it on their blogs. A blogger should try to become the first in covering top news and big websites like TechCrunch will list bloggers as the source.

High quality blogs get listed in Google news and bloggers can experiment with writing a blog which covers pictures only. Video blogging will become viral quickly and it will pave the way towards ravings fans of the blog. Bloggers should pay special attention to write fantastic headlines that grab the attention of readers. Creative bloggers submit their blog posts to social news sites like Sphinn (Now known as Marketing Land) and Bizsugar. Advertising the blog on Craigslist will bring massive traffic to the blog and reviewing products related to our niche on Amazon is another smart strategy to drive traffic.

Bloggers can consider reviewing websites related to their niche on Alexa and they can link back to their site in review. Blogging buffs can submit their blog posts to Digg (News aggregator site) and they should make sure that readers subscribe to their feed. Translating the content on our blog will lead to increased number of international visitors to the blog. The blog posts should be proofread regularly and starting a creative product or company related to the blog content is an innovative idea. Bloggers should use a highly functional Search Engine Optimization tool and it will lead to more links to the website.

Bloggers can make use of offline advertising methods like billboards and flyers and famous bloggers conduct free blogging seminar in their locality. Creating a survey about a popular topic will lead to more back links and traffic and the creation of a blog post that ranks people/things is another way to drive traffic to the blog. Avid bloggers should focus on creating elegant infographics which will ultimately drive traffic to their blog. Bloggers who have made huge amount of money through blogging have created free ebooks and they linked it back to their website. They can create free CSS templates and submit them to CSS directories with a link back to their blog.

Bloggers can think about creating great podcasts and submitting it to iTunes and it will position them as a thought leader in the industry. Successful bloggers will have a Facebook fan page of their blog and bloggers should necessarily do keyword research before writing a blog post. Creating a mobile version is an absolute must in today's world where everyone has a smartphone. Have you ever thought of creating an iPhone or Android app for your blog? There are chances of our blog's iPhone/Android app may become an instantaneous hit. Another wonderful way to bring traffic to the blog is the creation of a keyword rich HubPages (User generated content website) article.

As Google gives priority to websites with fresh content, it is recommended to update the blog as often as possible. Social media sites are the great traffic sources of blog and the title of blog post is important just like the content. An ideal blog title should entice readers and the readership will increase naturally and photos in blog post will increase readership. The keyword should be included in the ALT image tag on the photo and every blog page should have a keyword strategy. Keyword concentration helps search engines to understand what the page is about and videos bring more traffic to the blog as Google owns YouTube.

According to successful bloggers of contemporary age, videos in a blog post should be informative and entertaining. The blog shall be cross promoted to a mailing list and the content in a blog should be easy to read using sub headings, numbered lists and bullets. Kindle publishing is a smart strategy to attract targeted traffic to a website and Kindle books can be used to drive traffic to the blog by linking directly to the blog inside the book and using a free giveaway. This Kindle strategy will send around 200 extra visitors to the blog site within thirty days and a top ranked ebook will send around 2000 visitors a month. Giving free giveaway in Kindle is an easy and effective technique to attract web traffic within a short period of time.

How Does Blogging Help Small Businesses?

Blogging is a cost effective way of brand building and small businesses can immensely benefit from blogging. The objective of a business blog is to connect with potential customers, share expertise and drive more traffic. Blog builds a positive branding image and it makes a deep connection when compared with newsletter. Passionate entrepreneurs can write about their thoughts and passions in their blog and there are easy to use tools available for blogging. Blogs are of low cost when compared with websites and a blog gives us the freedom to post as often as we can.

Business blogging is a perfect way to connect with customers on a 24/7 basis and blogging generates feedback on products as well as services. A business blog often works as a recruiting tool and it builds credibility along with trustworthiness. Readers can respond to business blogs through questions, comments as well as shares and blogs are more search engine friendly than websites. Google will consider blog as a good reference for certain search terms if the blog produces good as well as fresh content. A blog is an essential tool to increase web presence and it gives small businesses an incredible opportunity to deliver their messages.

A business blog is a place where we find customers and some of us might ask the question "is blogging worth for small businesses". The answer is a big and blatant "Yes" and blogging on frequent basis is easy when compared to other online marketing methods. Quality business blog content increases visibility on Search Engine Results page and blogging helps our firm to establish the identity of a market leader. Small businesses competing with large companies can make use of blogging in an effective way. A business blog is a marketing channel that helps to support business growth and blogging helps businesses to get discovered through Social media.

Business blog serves as the ultimate repository of content and it helps to convert web traffic into leads. Every blog post is an opportunity to generate more leads and lead generating call to action should be included in a blog post. Blog call to actions lead to free ebooks, free reports, fact sheets, free webinars and not every blog visitor will turn into a lead. An ideal business blog answers common questions their customers have and businesses who are constantly creating quality content related to their niche will become an established authority. Majority of the internet marketers have rated blog content creation as their top most priority in 2018.

Blogging has become an essential component of marketing strategy and Mashable, Buzzfeed, Gizmodo and Venture Beat are the classic examples of business blogs. Most businesses use blogging as an effective way to drive traffic to their website and a business blog is about buyer persona. A business of today is judged by online interactions and business blogging is all about quality over quantity. Business blogs require a solid promotion strategy to get their content in front of different buyers. Search Engine Optimization (SEO) is crucial for business blogging and one of the most effective SEO techniques is to blog more frequently than competitors.

Business bloggers should keep in mind that eighty percent of internet users are searching for information through search engines. Creating relevant content on business blog refers to the practice of creating original content that addresses the questions of businesses. Content marketing is known as the new Search Engine Optimization and Google's webmaster guideline says, "Make sure that your site adds value. Provide unique and relevant content that gives users a reason to visit your site first". According to a HubSpot study, companies that published 16+ blog posts per month got three times more traffic than companies that published between 0-4 posts per month.

Higher blogging frequency benefits companies irrespective of their sizes and blogging frequently leads to more sales. The total number of indexed pages will go up as we publish more and more content in business blog. Organic traffic is a prized source of leads and business blogs should pursue all possible avenues to get more subscribers to their blog. A business blog should be located on the same domain of the website such as blog.domain.com or domain.com/blog. Business blog readers like consistency and bloggers should pay attention to implement a routine publishing schedule.

Publishing blog article about a current business topic is a great way to bring more traffic to the blog site. Social share button is an essential component of business blogging and social sharing buttons can increase click through rates by fifty five percent. A clear call to action should be included in each and every blog post of a business blog and the business blog should be perceived as a way to educate buyer persona. The business blog should be optimized for speed and the speed of website can be checked using online tools like webpagetest.org. An ideal business blog should be optimized for Smartphones as well as tablets as the contemporary era witnesses rapid increase in the usage of mobile internet.

The keyword in a business blog should be featured in page titles, headers, alt tags and images. Proper usage of keywords increases opportunity to rank high in search engines very significantly. Business bloggers should ensure that they link to relevant content in their blog post and name as well as photo can be included in a business blog post. Most business blogs and websites will have "Write for Us" and "Work with Us" sections. Guest blogging is the better way to start out in business blogging and building portfolio is the easiest part of business blogging.

Contently.com is a perfect platform to create our first business blog portfolio and small companies make the ultimate use of business blogging. The writing style in a business blog should be on a personal level and business bloggers should try their best to establish significant relationship with their customers. Business blog writer should focus on relevant research, thought, responding to posts from readers, and frequent updates. All business bloggers should ask themselves the following questions.

What type of content will be posted on the business blog?

Do we want the blog to make important announcements and promote special events?

Do we want to share news on special promotions?

Improving the Credibility of Blog

It is often said that blogging is about showcasing expertise in a particular niche and readers who find the information on blog useful will become repeat visitors. The subscribers of a typical blog will sign up to newsletter, RSS feed, and comment on the blog post. Building a popular blog is about building online credibility and the first step to improve the credibility of blog is to become a subject matter expert. Bloggers should try their best to improve the credibility of blog and good design adds to the credibility of a blog. Blogging masters opine that the information given in a blog post should be accurate and well written.

An ideal blog should be devoid of factual errors and making an error decreases the credibility of our blog. Bloggers should try to avoid articles on subjects which they are less familiar and having grammatical errors in a blog post will keep away prospective readers. The articles in a blog should look absolutely professional and bloggers should edit them multiple times. Getting a custom blog theme is a super way to improve the credibility of blog and a custom blog theme helps a blog to look more professional. Custom blog design allows customizing the navigation and layout of the blog which makes it more user friendly.

A custom blog theme will be costlier than generic theme and internet's most successful blogs have custom design. The best benefit of custom theme is that it offers exclusivity and custom blog theme will become a necessity as the blog expands. Keywords should not be overused in a typical blog post and blog posts should remain readable and interesting. Bloggers should focus on placing keywords evenly through the body of post and synonyms or variations of the keywords can be used to avoid repetition. Avid bloggers should try to get links from credible blogs and it will work wonders for Search Engine Optimization too.

Building the credibility of blog is a process which takes time and statistics and data can be cited in a blog post. Testimonials and reviews will help to increase the credibility of a blog immensely and a blog should be simple to navigate. One of the best ways to improve the credibility of a blog is to provide quality information and the information should matter to prospective visitors. The contact information in a blog should be easy to find and creating a separate contact information page is an excellent idea. Bloggers of today should recognize that blogs are influential than traditional websites and every blogger should turn him or herself into a credible blogger.

Readers should trust blogger with each and every word and consistency and persistence are the characteristics of credible blog. Community building should be the main focus of blogging and bloggers should prioritize high quality content over content created to make money. A blogger should have his own view and opinion and all thoughts of a blogger should be backed up by logic. An ideal blog post should be meaningful and interactions should be valuable and each blog post should represent personality of the blogger. A credible blogger should have the mindset of giving back to the community and the saying, "the more you give, the more you will receive" is applicable to blogging too.

Blogging is a great way of getting natural links and it is the best way of building relationships with online entities. Some bloggers treat blogging as a purely link building activity and blog can be used as an effective tool for building credibility, authority and influence. An ideal blog should be in sync with principles and values of business and the blog content should always bring something new to the readers. Readers expect a new and different perspective in all blog posts and the quality of blog post should never be compromised. A blog should address a particular need of their target audience and a blog post should necessarily be a solutions provider.

Blogs are considered as a great way to build online credibility and the most important factors that add credibility to a blog are quality content, regular content publishing, good authors, high quality testimonials, good design, excellent social media presence and high number of subscribers. The social media presence or influence of a blog can be measured by high number of social media blog post shares, social media mentions, and increased number of social media followers. Facebook, Twitter, Google Plus, LinkedIn and Pinterest add the maximum credibility to a blog in the current age of social media revolution. Bloggers should increase their presence on social networks and they should gain more followers. According to recent survey reports, multiple authors add credibility to a blog or website.

Guest post will help blogs to attract new audiences, build relationships and receive quality content from experts in the field. Articles, infographics, visuals, graphs, charts, audio, podcast interviews, ebooks, video and webinar in blog posts add more credibility. Ebooks are often distributed in blog posts in the form of white papers, guides as well as reports. The list of most credible blog content include case study, news, interviews, surveys, how to articles, stories and reviews. Bad content, fake social media followers, advertisement, less number of subscribers, and bad design destroy the credibility of a blog.

Must Have Plug-ins for Home Business WordPress Blog

The essential WordPress plug-ins for home business WordPress blog are Akismet, Social Bookmarking Links plug-in, Google sitemaps plug-in, and Google AdSense. Akismet is a WordPress plug-in which checks whether the comments look like spam and it allows bloggers to review the comments before approving it. WordPress.com API key is needed to activate Akismet and it works perfectly like computer anti-spam software. Social bookmarking links plug-in links to favourite social bookmarking sites on pages, posts and RSS feeds. Google sitemap will create XML sitemap of WordPress blog and it supports all WordPress generated pages.

Google sitemap gets updated automatically and all major search engines will be notified about the new update. Google AdSense is a maintenance free method of generating passive income from the blog and bloggers should have an approved AdSense account from Google. One great feature of WordPress is that we can install all types of special plug-ins to create a powerful blog or website. Most WordPress plug-ins are available for free and plug-ins like Sitemap Generator can be installed very quickly. A sitemap generator plug-in allows to create special sitemaps meant for search engines and sitemaps are helpful in getting the web page indexed by search engines. "All in One SEO" plug-in is another popular WordPress plug-in and it is used to increase web traffic.

Plug-ins are the reason why we should self host a WordPress blog and the two essential WordPress plug-ins are Easy privacy policy and Sociable. "All in One SEO Pack" helps us to define titles, keywords as well as descriptions for each post. It ensures that site traffic reaches our site and Sociable prompts visitors to make their content viral. Price is an important factor while buying an auto blogging plug-in for WordPress and auto blogging plug-in for WordPress supports automatic content generation from article directories. WordPress automatic plug-in software allows integration of media content from places like YouTube and Flickr.

Some automated blog solutions support affiliate programs and a fully integrated autoblogging plug-in is an essential feature of WordPress blog. BuddyPress plug-ins for WordPress blogs are quite popular and it plays a pivotal role in enhancing the user experience. The plug-in of BuddyPress is helpful in creating social networking websites and this plug-in allows registering on a site to create profile. BuddyPress is compatible up to WordPress 3.6 version and Events Manager is a feature rich event registration management solution for WordPress. Flexibility and reliability are the inbuilt powerful features of Events Manager BuddyPress plug-in. Fast Secure Contact Form plug-in works as a customizable contact form and webmasters can easily create contact forms using this plug-in.

Rating Widget is a WordPress plug-in which helps with social connects and it allows users to easily create ratings using the WordPress dashboard. Welcome Pack WordPress plug-in allows sending invites and welcoming messages automatically. Email customization facility is another top rung feature of Welcome Pack and Author Avatars List is another WordPress plug-in which shows lists of user avatars. Single avatars can be easily inserted using User Avatars List and Twit Connect is a fantastic BuddyPress plug-in for WordPress. Another WordPress plug-in called as Envolve Chat works as a customizable chat toolbar and it can be added to the WordPress blog community.

BuddyPress group email subscription is a WordPress plug-in which allows receiving of email notifications. Groupblog plug-in helps in the extension of group functionality and the facility of automated blog registration is offered in Groupblog. Plug-ins convert the blog into a high powered online tool and Page Mash is a WordPress page management plug-in. The AJAX interface of Page Mash allows drag and drop pages put into the order we like and WP Super Cache is a WordPress plug-in which improves the performance of website. The WordPress plug-in of NextGEN image gallery is useful in showing a series of product images and publishing slideshow.

Gravity forms is a superb WordPress plug-in for managing online forums and the list of most popular Twitter plug-ins for WordPress include WPtouch, AddThis, WordBooker, Social Media Widget, Network Publisher, podPress, and User Access Manager. WPtouch converts WordPress blog into iPhone application and it is excellent for AJAX driven loading of site. It makes sure that WordPress blog gets transformed into a stylish mobile version and AddThis is a social bookmarking widget for bookmarking. A user can easily share and bookmark a site using AddThis and it can be used with more than three hundred bookmarking services. WordBooker enables cross posting and cross posting can be done as an Extract, Note or Status update.

Users can add links to social media and site profiles using Social Media Widget, another well known WordPress plug-in. Network Publishers lets us to publish blog posts automatically to social networks including Twitter, Facebook and LinkedIn. podPress eases the task of hosting a podcast and it supports automatic feed generation facility too. User Access Manager plug-in empowers users with the ability to easily manage access to their posts, files as well as pages. Google Analytics for WordPress is an essential plug-in for every blogger and The Yet Another Related Post Plug-in is an excellent tool for keeping visitors on the site longer.

WP DB Manager is another essential WordPress plug-in and it allows backing up database and automatic scheduling feature is a prominent attraction of WP DB Manager. Platinum SEO Pack is another well known SEO plug-in for WordPress blog and other popular WordPress plug-ins are Thesis and Optimize Press. "Share This" is a prominent plug-in for WordPress blogs and the WordPress plug-in of SEO smart links provide automatic SEO benefits. WordPress SEO by Yoast is a popular plug-in which helps in sitemap generation and it retains the functionality of SEO sitemaps. WordPress SEO by Yoast is compatible up to the version of WordPress 3.5.1 and Mingle Forum is another WordPress plug-in which enables simple putting up of a forum.

WP Mingle is the simple way to turn WordPress website into a social network and it uses standard WordPress website and themes. The exquisite features of Mingle are User Profile Pages, ability to upload custom avatars, friend activity pages, email notifications, Twitter like user tagging and custom profile fields. WP Auctions is an innovative ecommerce plug-in for WordPress and it allows hosting auctions on websites for free. Artpal is another famous shopping plug-in for WordPress and artists can sell their works using Artpal. Easy PayPal integration is the striking attraction of Artpal and it offers real time sales update.

Effective Blog Writing Styles

The ultimate objective of blogging is to deliver compelling and informative content and the first rule of blogging is that the content should be always fresh. Originality is the second most important feature of blog posts and blogs with fascinating topics and elegant writing style will attract more audience. An ideal blog should be interesting to the target audience and different types of blogging styles are brand blogging, link blogging, video blogging, photo blogging, list blogging, event blogging, insight blogging, and review blogging. Brand blog is the blog about a typical brand, product or service and it offers an informative look at the brand.

Brand blogging should necessarily include positive features of the product and link blogging is a compilation of group of links. Link blogging serves as a resource list and video blogging is an effective marketing tool since videos are appealing. Photo blogging is a fantastic blogging approach and readers find list blogging as extremely useful. Event blogging is the blogging about different events including conferences, seminars and workshops. Insight blogging shares ideas, thoughts, and discussions of trends in a particular topic and it is a more formal approach to blogging. Response blogging is the direct response to a question or challenge and bloggers start a discussion in meme blogging by responding to a question.

Meme blogging promotes interesting and exciting discussions about a particular topic and review blogging is the blogging where we give opinion on a new product and service. Guest blogging promotes great deal of discussion and both the writer and reader will benefit from guest blogging. In interview blogging, bloggers can publish an audio or video interview and they can publish transcript from the interview. Persuasive and clear communication is the primary objective of every blog and website of today. Short paragraphs like the ones seen in newspapers should be used in blogs and using short sentences in blog posts is recommended.

Bloggers should use simple words in a blog post and they should be specific and to the point. Blogging fans should read a lot in order to develop good writing skills and an enthusiastic writing style will get noticed by readers. Bloggers should keep in mind their brand and audience while writing blog content and long sentences should be avoided in a blog post. Blog writers should use the synonym if they use the same word many times and metaphors can be used in a blog. Using expressions is a great way to spice up text and a listicle is a bulleted blog post which gives a list of reasons, ideas and products.

The first sentence of a blog post should make readers curious and bloggers should have a clear understanding of their target audience. The starting topic of a blog can be general and the blog title should give enough information about the blog topic. Bloggers should focus on changing the topic scope, adjusting the time frame, choosing a new audience, and introducing a new format. The introduction of the blog post should be really captivating and bloggers should ensure that readers are not getting intimidated by the length of content. Sub sections make the content in a blog post easy to read and outlining the post is the first step of blog writing.

The blog post outline should be used as an introductory guide and some recommended tools for blog writing are Power Thesaurus, Zen Pen, and Cliché Finder. Power Thesaurus provides bloggers with tons of alternative word choices and the editing process is an important component of blogging. Bloggers should choose a visually appealing image for their blog and social networks give more importance to content with images. It has been pointed out that content with relevant images receive 94 percent more views than content without images. Formatting and organization of the post are extremely important and the writing style should stay consistent from post to post.

Tags allow blog readers to browse for more content in the same niche and bloggers should choose 10-20 tags for each blog post. A call to action should be inserted at the end of blog post and the most common call to action options are subscribing to the blog, downloading ebook, registering for webinar or read another related article. Call to action is a valuable resource for the person reading our content and every blog post should be optimized for on page SEO. The blog post URL (Uniform Resource Locator) should be made shorter and keyword friendly. Meta description of a blog post should be between 150-160 characters and they should start with a verb including "Learn" and "Discover".

Post title is the most important on page SEO factor and bloggers shouldn't overcomplicate their title with keywords. Bloggers should make use of every opportunity to add keywords and the headlines should be kept under sixty five characters. Blog writers can consider linking to pages they want to rank well for the keyword and an ideal blog of today should be mobile optimized. Bloggers should definitely pick a catchy title and all blog posts are built around Search Engine Optimized keywords. Casual writing style is recommended for blogs and blog posts of today have begun to have more interviews and in-depth articles.

As blogs all over the world have become more professional, they have started hiring editors for the publication. Blogs of contemporary age are opinion driven write ups from industry leaders and article style blog posts enjoy more authority. Successful blog posts are creatively conceptualized write ups and larger font provides audience with a great reading experience. The blog post should be limited to two to three sentences per paragraph and bloggers should give importance to the use of bold texts. Bold text makes skimming and scanning through the articles lot easier and styling blog post will make it more appealing.

According to blogging aficionados, bloggers can use other types of font styles such as italics and strikethroughs. The purpose of bold and italics in blog post is to differentiate keywords from rest of the paragraph. Many bloggers consider insight blogging as the most difficult type of blogging to do and ambition bloggers target decision makers through the blog post. Piggyback blogging is writing about a topic that is popular in the news media and life blogging includes a blog post sharing the story of something that happened in personal life. The most important thing as far as announcement blogging is concerned is being the first to break the news.

Home Business and Blog Marketing

The objective of blog marketing is promoting the blog in order to get more readers and blog owners use affiliate links to sell products and services of merchants. A blogger should have multiple blogs to do the blog marketing effectively and taking care of the aspirations of blog readers is the crucial aspect of blog marketing. Bloggers should ensure that their blog is relevant and a blog marketer should know about things they are going to advertise. Blog marketer should have a crystal clear idea of increasing the ranking of the blog in search engine results. Effective Search Engine Optimization strategies will lead to more traffic and leads from the blog.

Many blog marketers outsource majority of their works and bloggers should start with small goals. Blogging often acts as a cost effective way to get traffic to the home business website and blogging itself will be a home based business. Blog marketing helps to keep connected with our target audience and the most important aspect of blog marketing is the creation of evergreen content. According to blogging experts, an ideal blog post should be content relevant and topic driven. Bloggers should incorporate SEO tips into blogging and loading content with keywords will put down the quality of blog post.

Bloggers can use the keyword and its variations in title and description of a typical blog post. They can create promotions, surveys, quizzes and contests for home based business and social media can be effectively used for the blog promotion. Pay per Click advertising methods can be used for blog promotion and there is a search engine optimization benefit if we host the blog as a sub directory of the main company domain name. Using the blog software as a content management system is an efficient way to manage the website content. Bloggers should have a clear idea about the following things before starting a blog.

Does the blog serve as a journal for starting the business?

Is the blog a search marketing tool?

Is the blog used to create credibility?

Will the blog serve as the main company website?

A blog should serve as company website, landing page host, small business resource and marketing tool. Most blog hosting solutions allow a sub directory such as companysite.com/blog and the dedicated domain name will work better if the blog is independent of the primary company brand. Blogs should have a catchy and significant brand name and a Linux hosting account is available for $10-$20 per month.

A specialist should take care of the maintenance, addition of plug-ins, design as well as functionality updates of a blog. Blog design should be modified to suit the branding and design customization includes modifying the CSS, JavaScript and graphics. The next set of customization includes plug-ins to improve the front end functionality as well as search engine friendliness. The recommended plug-ins for WordPress blog are Redirection, Posts2Posts, CommentLuv, Members Only and FeedSmith Feed burner plug-in. Every blogger should create a content plan and common keyword research tools for blogging include Google Keyword Planner, Word Tracker, and KeywordDiscovery.com.

Being responsive is an essential blog marketing strategy and the social bookmarking tools are great for adding functionality to a web page. The blog and its RSS feed can be submitted to RSS directories including Alltop, Blogdir, Blogflux, and Bloghub. Bloggers should essentially set up social profiles in sites including Facebook, Twitter and LinkedIn. The tool TwitterFeed can be used to publish the latest blog post to Twitter automatically and the blog URL should be published everywhere we publish the website address. Blog measurement is focused on web analytics and standard tools like Google Analytics will address our needs. Bloggers make use of social media monitoring tools like Techrigy SM2, Scoutlabs and Radian6.

A business blog helps to cement our position as an expert in the field and an ideal business blog should provide excellent content including news, tips and trends. A business blog often functions as a content marketing hub and business blog is a long term commitment. Bloggers should recognize that business blog is an investment of time, energy as well as effort. Blogging enthusiasts should ask themselves the below given questions before starting a business blog.

Why am I starting a blog?

Who is my target audience?

The purpose of a business blog should be reader centered and bloggers need to know who their target audience is before creating killer content. Consistency is the most important component of business blogging and many business blogs are written by more than two bloggers. Business blogs will immensely benefit from guest bloggers and developing an editorial calendar is the preliminary stage of business blogging. Editorial calendar is essential to maintain content strategy and design, colours and font size of a business blog will make or break it. Businesses all over the world use blogs to promote their business, share news with customers, reach new audiences and generate sales. Speed and ability to engage with readers make blogging the perfect marketing tool of contemporary age.

Blogging experts point out that managing a business blog needs planning, resourcing and monitoring. Business bloggers should know how blogs work, benefits of business blogs, and ideas for better blogging. A business blog serves as an extension of business website and a high quality business blog is a set of regular updates that prompt readers to come back again. The content of a business blog is continuously updated in a diary format and many business blogs contain photographs, video, audio and music. One of the most effective usages of a blog is providing an interactive experience for its readers.

Allowing readers to leave comments on the blog will create an online conversation and the dash board is a common part of business blog which is accessible only to the blog authors. The dashboard gives access to changing the look of blog design, managing posts and reviewing them. Each business blog can be categorized and tagged keywords will help readers to find posts that interest them. Blog entries in a business blog can be organized into archives which readers can browse by selecting a particular date, month or year. Storage and backup of blog entries is an unavoidable part of contemporary business blogging arena.

How to Create WordPress blog for Internet Business Opportunity?

A WordPress blog is a very simple method of promoting individual internet business and WordPress blog entries are displayed in reverse chronological order. WordPress blogs provide commentary on a particular subject and a typical WordPress post combines text, links and comments. Micro blogging is another type of blogging which features short posts and some personal WordPress blogs have gained huge popularity.

Blogging Action Steps

Sign up for WordPress account

Select a theme

Elect a hosting account

Write the first blog post

WordPress is the easiest and user friendly application for blogging and WordPress.com is often called as web 2.0 site. The web hosting company we choose should have years of experience with WordPress and WP Engine is a company which specializes in WordPress. Bluehost is the recommended WordPress web hosting solution and an ideal web hosting plan should give bloggers unlimited domains/websites. Script installer such as Fantastico or Softaculous can be used for the installation of WordPress. WordPress acts as the best blogging software for newbies as well as professionals and the biggest advantage of WordPress is that it has no limitations. WordPress is undoubtedly a cost efficient blogging platform and strong support community is another prominent attraction of WordPress.

WordPress CMS allows the usage of affiliate links, Google AdSense and cost per action opt-in forms. It has changed the way people blog and WordPress automatically updates the blog whenever the site gets updated. Creating, maintaining and managing the blog are pretty easy with the one and only WordPress CMS. WordPress does all the hard work for blogger and it is the most professional blog publishing application. Self hosted WordPress allows bloggers to download, install and host the free WordPress platform.

A self hosted WordPress blog provides the highest level of customization and it features infinite options to earn revenue. Bloggers can add shopping carts, widgets and plug-ins for click through using the majestic WordPress. Free, customized and premium themes available in WordPress give it a professional look and feel. Bloggers will have total control over the WordPress and WordPress allows every single page to be search engine indexed. Creating a unique domain is the crucial step of building a WordPress blog and bloggers will have to connect WordPress to their hosting account. The next step is to configure WordPress settings and WordPress users will be provided with their own server space. Self hosted WordPress blog allows choosing the right hosting package that meets our requirements.

WordPress is the most versatile blogging platform available today and non techies will need little bit of help in the initial stage of setting up their WordPress blog. It has been rated as the perfect blogging platform for business blogs for the design, functionality and SEO. Premium WordPress themes are available at ThemeForest and an ideal WordPress theme should be responsive. WordPress theme should display properly on different devices including PC, tablet, and smartphone. WordPress themes should come with proper customer support and an ideal WordPress theme allows changing colours, navigation menu and buttons.

Domain name can be bought from domain registrars including NameCheap, 1&1, and GoDaddy. The domain name will cost around $10 per year and bloggers should pay attention to choosing a .com domain name. Domain name should be easy to remember and top providers of web hosting are GoDaddy, HostGator, and Bluehost. The objective of WordPress blogging is often to get more leads, build email list and become an expert in the field. Most WordPress based business blogs are equipped with email opt-in box, link to sales page or Call to Action. There are some fantastic WordPress plug-ins that help us to optimize, audit and promote the site including Sharebar.

WordPress dashboard is the summary of things on the blog and posts will be the most used area of dashboard. Bloggers can upload images on WordPress and the most prominent image websites are iStock photo, Pixabay and Picjumbo. WordPress web hosting packages normally cost $8 per month. Bluehost is the largest brand name in WordPress web hosting and WordPress login URL will look like http://yoursite.com/wp-admin. The visual appearance of WordPress is controlled by themes and bloggers can change their theme by clicking on Appearance>Themes.

Each WordPress theme caters to a different market and WordPress theme should complement the content of our website. Simplicity is the first and foremost quality of a WordPress theme and theme's presentation style shouldn't be over complicated. Google shows mobile friendly WordPress pages on the top of their search results and most WordPress themes of today are responsive by default. WordPress theme should be compatible with different browsers including Mozilla Firefox, Apple Safari, Google Chrome, and Internet Explorer. An ideal WordPress theme should support all popular plug-ins and it should ideally support multilingual WordPress sites. Page builders are WordPress plug-ins that allow us to create page layouts and many WordPress themes come with page builders preinstalled.

Bloggers should ensure that they select a WordPress theme which has good documentation and support options. Some premium WordPress themes offer detailed documentation with email support and WordPress theme plays a major role in determining the SEO friendliness. Bloggers can check if the page generates proper HTML5 by checking it with W3C Markup validation service. Ratings and reviews are other indicators of WordPress themes and some of the highly recommended WordPress theme shops are Themify, Elegant Themes, StudioPress and ArrayThemes. World's most talented photographers, designers, and artists use WordPress to display their fantastic artworks.

Portfolio Gallery is a well known free WordPress photography theme and it is equipped with multiple page templates. Aperture is a fully responsive WordPress theme and the full screen slider of Aperture displays photographs on our home page. Tography Lite is a WordPress theme designed for photography blogs and it focuses on image as well as typography. Photo Session is a responsive WordPress theme and its major features are full screen slider and navigation menus. Divina is a free WordPress theme used by photographers, fashion blogs and fashion websites. Photo World is a WooCommerce ready photography theme for WordPress and it comes with thumbnail displays. Lens is a WordPress theme which is ideal for photographers, designers as well as advertising companies.

Tips to Launch a Professional Blog

The best blogging software for professional blog is definitely the WordPress and powerful features, tons of templates and flexibility to customize the blog are the top rated attractions of WordPress. Professional blog should have a standalone domain name and it should include RSS subscription options, social bookmarking links, title tags and sitemap. It has been pointed out that fresh content in professional blog is welcomed by both readers and search engines alike. Posting as a guest blogger is another way to market a professional blog and guest bloggers should submit their blog post to blogs with large number of followers. Many youngsters have jumped into the blogging world to earn a nice part time income and professional blogging is about owning a self hosted WordPress blog.

WordPress allows extending its basic capabilities and it is quite easy to learn WordPress in our pursuit of creating professional blog. An ideal professional blog should be well maintained as well as well branded and professional blog should be treated like real business. Many professional blogs make use of Thesis WordPress theme and it ensures quick loading of the website. Thesis theme is equipped with built-in responsive design and many top professional blogs use the WordPress theme "The Genesis Framework". Readers expect value from a professional website and professional blog writers can write, podcast, or record videos about their topic.

Longer blog posts are recommended in a professional blog and professional blogs should essentially start a newsletter. Many professional bloggers use the services of Aweber for newsletter creation and professional bloggers should set up their profile in leading social media channels including Facebook, Twitter, LinkedIn and Pinterest. Easy social share button is an essential component of professional blogs and the "Start here" page should consist of quick summary of what the webpage is about, a list of most popular articles and sign-up forms. Ninja popup plug-in allows creating popup windows that show up in front of the content and it helps readers to sign up for newsletter. Professional blogs should install WordPress security plug-ins such as WordFence, Bulletproof Security, Sucuri Security, iThemes Security and Acunetix WP Security Scan.

Professional blogs should have a catchy headline and few of the best templates for elegant headlines include simple steps, smart ways and quick and smart guide to X (refers to the topic). Professional blog should be accompanied with an appealing image taken from websites like Flickr and Unsplash. Bullet points, images and sub titles can be used in a professional blog just to make it look more captivating. Professional bloggers can add "Frequently Asked Questions" section to their blog and criticism should not hold back professional bloggers.

The five simple steps of launching a professional blog are getting the web hosting, picking the domain name, setting up WordPress, creating content and building traffic. Professional blogs are often equipped with less casual voice and the popularity of professional blogs has skyrocketed in the recent years. Getting started with a professional blog is very cheap and professional bloggers don't need to be technical geniuses. Twitter can be effectively used to promote professional blog and content marketing has become increasingly popular in the contemporary world of intense business competition. Almost every estore or online service of today will have their own blog and it underlines the importance of professional blogging.

Blogs help professionals to increase their online presence, develop an audience, send traffic to the website and promote products. Twenty five percent of today's websites are powered by WordPress and updating a professional blog with WordPress is quite easy. The advent of WordPress has made blog creation intuitive as well as user friendly and Weebly is another amazing website builder for professional blogs. WordPress users will have more tools at their disposal and WordPress.com is much more limited when compared to WordPress.org. Every web hosting company of today supports WordPress and web hosting will make or break a professional blog.

Cost, speed, uptime and technical support are the most important factors as far as web hosting of professional blog is concerned. Good web hosting company will help to avoid problems with downtime and shared hosting is the most basic type of web hosting available. Cloud hosting will offer faster website speeds since it stores websites across multiple shared servers. It has been found that cloud hosting increases site performance and VPS hosting is recommended for websites with huge traffic. WordPress hosting offered by web hosting companies will give the seamless WordPress experience.

Bloggers looking for cheap hosting can select the basic shared hosting plan and the WordPress hosting of Bluehost is built on VPS technology. The content delivery network offered by Bluehost provides faster website loading and WordPress optimized plans of Bluehost start at $20 per month. Bluehost has been rated as a reliable provider of web hosting for professional blogs and their cheap shared hosting plan is great for professional blogs. The shared hosting plan of Bluehost start at $2.95 per month and their virtual private server hosting is priced at $19.99. WP Engine provides high end WordPress hosting for small businesses and it starts at $29 per month.

Professional bloggers with more than 20000 visitors per month can make use of WP Engine and WP Engine's hosting plans are the best for companies with multiple blogs. Domain name is the first point of contact the audience will have with our professional blog. Bluehost offers free domain when we sign up to their shared hosting plan and GoDaddy is the world's biggest domain name registrar. Five minute installation is the most talked about attraction of WordPress and a premium WordPress theme will allow to control every aspect of the website. WordPress has its own collection of free themes including Twenty Seventeen, Twenty Sixteen and Twenty Fifteen.

Free WordPress themes allow bloggers to play with different colour schemes as well as layouts. According to well known blogging enthusiasts, premium themes offer a stylish and professional look. The price of premium WordPress themes range from $29 to $99 and the installation of too many plug-ins will slow down WordPress. Out of date WordPress plug-ins are a security risk and poorly coded plug-ins should be avoided at all costs. Many WordPress web hosting companies offer back up for their customers and Duplicator is an automatic WordPress plug-in for the backup functionality. Bloggers integrate Google Analytics to WordPress for tracking website visitors and the ideal length of a blog post in professional blog is 1000+ words.

WordPress Blog

WordPress is the professional and great way to start a blog and WordPress blog is a powerful tool for publishing on the internet. It uses programming languages called PHP and MySQL, a database used to display content. Creating a WordPress blog is super easy and Site Ground is another recommended hosting provider of WordPress. Site Ground charges $62 per year for WordPress hosting and there are thousands of third party themes available at WordPress.org. WordPress blog is great for SEO purposes and the built-in SEO wizard of WordPress blog helps to get indexed in search engines like Google, Yahoo, and Bing.

It is very easy to setup an online store in WordPress blog with the elegant WooCommerce. Facebook, Twitter, YouTube and other social sites sharing buttons can be easily installed in a WordPress blog. Some WordPress blogs are equipped with email marketing apps and it allows sending promotional campaigns and newsletters. Digital payment solutions are available in WordPress and hosting packages of notable hosting companies come with WordPress preinstalled. WordPress is considered as a standard website creation tool all over the world and WordPress blog focuses on aesthetics, web standards and usability. It is an open source web platform and WordPress community offers free support at http://wordpress.org/support/.

WordPress hosting platforms offer extra security as well as managed services and hosting plans are connected to the latest versions of WordPress. WordPress.org was started in 2003 as a basic blogging platform and it eventually evolved into a full fledged content management system. Great control and added security are the peculiar features of WordPress hosting offered by NameCheap. The WordPress blog dashboard allows creating blog posts, changing the appearance of sites, widgets, and managing users. WordPress hosting services like WPX and Kinsta have good backup systems and a free plug-in called Updraftplus is available for backups.

Bloggers can change colours, backgrounds, fonts, menus and widgets using the WordPress customizer. The WordPress themes available at Thrive Themes are conversion focused and the possibilities of personalizing a WordPress site are endless. The list of advertising management plug-ins for WordPress include Ads Pro plug-in, WP Pro advertising system, WP in Post Ads, WP Quads, and AdRotate. Bloggers should not do compromise on the quality of web hosting service and shared hosting is the recommended option for WordPress blogs. Free WordPress themes miss many important aspects of premium WordPress themes and WordPress blogging of today is about self branding. WordPress blog is perfect for business owners, designers, web developers, SEO consultants and authors.

Adding ALT tags to images is very simple in WordPress and every WordPress blog post should have a clear call to action. It could be like "Read more posts like these" and "Signup for our newsletter". Broken Link Checker is a WordPress plug-in which monitors all internal links and reports on where they are. WordPress blog gives the ultimate control over HTML, CSS, image attributes, design as well as URL structure. The hosting options in WordPress are more economical for small businesses and Woo Commerce is maintained by the WordPress team. Most WordPress hosts make the integration of PayPal easy and WordPress is recommended to grow the business beyond startup stages.

WordPress is perfect for building dynamic and multipage site and the specialties of InMotion web hosting are unlimited disk space, ability to host unlimited sites on a single account, and preinstalled WordPress. YouTube videos are popular marketing methods for blogs and Bluehost hosts over 850000 WordPress blogs.

Popular websites which have used WordPress

The Walt Disney Company

Greenwich Library

Travel Portland

Captain Creative

Jess Marks Photography

The Walt Disney Company features a professional and simple WordPress website and the WordPress website of Greenwich Library has adopted a modern look. The colour coded navigation elements in the website of Greenwich Library takes us to the world of visual euphoria.

Pay per Click (PPC) is the easiest form of monetization for a WordPress blog and some PPC companies pay for page impressions. WordPress blog users can add plug-ins like Ad Inserter to place ads on their website and WordPress blog needs to have a good number of visitors to profit from Google AdSense. WordPress themes including Numinous Pro, Mugu Pro and Metro Magazine Pro have ad blockers. Pay per click is an easy passive income which can be made using WordPress blogs and WordPress is the ideal option for someone creating his/her first website. Large websites like Time Magazine, TechCrunch, CNN and NBC make use of the feature rich WordPress.

Most of the products associated with WordPress are easy to use and a domain name for business would be YourCompanyName.com. The most popular domain name extension is .com and short domain names often work better when compared with longer ones. Shared hosting and managed WordPress hosting are two popular hosting options for a typical WordPress blog. A site specific WordPress plug-in allows to add code snippets to WordPress website without relying on the theme. Custom WordPress themes will have unique design, layout as well as set of features. In order to create a custom WordPress theme, we need someone who can design and code our theme.

Page titles in WordPress are an important element for search engines and SEO optimization software like Scribe can be used to edit the page title as well as description. Keyword should be added in the image title and alternate text fields of a WordPress blog and Prose from StudioPress is the favourite theme of WordPress bloggers. Pineapple is another elegant WordPress theme used by thousands of bloggers and the best fonts for WordPress blogs are Arial and Verdana. Affordable images for WordPress blog can be found at websites like Big Stock and Death to Stock. Some knowledge of HTML is ideal for a WordPress blogger and a WordPress.org blog will be the sole property of blogger.

WordPress website is the best option for numerous online money making activities including running advertisements, marketing, selling products and offering memberships. The success of a WordPress blog is largely determined by the theme and Thrive Themes is the perfect option for sales funnel and lead capture. Bloggers should select a WordPress theme which looks good on Smartphones and it is good to use premium themes since many free themes have formatting issues with mobile devices. WP Touch Pro is the recommended plug-in for creating a mobile site and WP Beginner is a great resource for bloggers. WordPress bloggers should have a basic understanding of search engine optimization, usability and links.

How to Advertise Blogs Using Blog Directories?

An excellent way to advertise blog is by using the mailing list and bloggers should submit their blogs to different blog directories. Bloggers should submit blogs under the most suitable categories and submitting the blog to blog directories is an effective way to get quality back links. Advertising blogs using blog directories is the cost effective way to promote blogs and "Best of the Web Blog Search" is a powerful tool for sharing blog. EatonWebBlogDirectory is another well known blog directory and it costs $35 for the blog review. OnToplist.com is a free blog directory that reads the RSS feed of blog and it is powered with social sharing features, article directories and great tools.

BlogSearchEngine is a selective blog search engine and it comes with paid membership feature. Blog catalog consists of vast number of categories including "academic" and "writing". Bloggapedia has an interesting home page and their readers are easily connected to blogs as well as new posts. Spillbean is another blog directory with categories such as health, internet and personal. Blogging Fusion is a blog directory with over sixty categories and it has good number of listings too. Blogarama has an extensive collection of blogs and blog directories help bloggers to expose their blog to large number of audience.

Blog directories are frequently crawled by search engines including Yahoo, MSN and Google. The structure of blog directories is most suitable for search engines and search engine optimization. It is to be pointed out that most blog directories get huge traffic and they will have large number of inbound links. Majority of the blog directories provide RSS feed updates and RSS feed makes it easy for individuals to subscribe to the blog feed. Blog directory submission software has made the task of submitting blogs to directories an easy one. Blog directories will ask the blog owner to provide the URL for RSS feed and they have become an important location for blog search.

Ping is a tool which enables bloggers to notify blog directories and it is a quick transmission to the blog directory. Pings will send blogs to the top of updated blog lists and the use of an automated tool is the easiest way to ping directories. Pingomatic is a well known ping tool for blogs and WordPress is setup to notify Pingomatic as soon as a post is published. Web traffic is a vital part of any blogging campaign and Midnight Bloggers is an awesome blog directory integrated with ClickBank and Google AdSense. The most common features of popular blog directories are blogs, author profile as well as links.

WordPress dashboard is the place where we start building, managing and maintaining WordPress blog or website. A professional WordPress blog will showcase our skills, provide details of experience and give clients a way to get in touch. WordPress is the easy to understand, easy to work with and the most easily adaptable Content Management System. The best method to advertise WordPress blog is definitely the blog directories and it features WYSIWYG (What You See is What You Get) editor. Prestigious organizations like Reuters and Spotify use WordPress Content Management System for their websites.

Paying for a premium WordPress theme guarantees high quality, excellent performance and continued support. Bloggers can check "Woo Themes" and "Get Your Themes" for dazzling WordPress themes at affordable price tags. Standard WordPress widgets include links to websites, automatic list of pages and a calendar of posts. Some blog directories charge a fee for blog submission and some of them offer both free and paid options. The objective of a blog search engine is finding blog entries that match specific keywords and blog search engines will have huge databases. Dmoz.org is one of the most popular blog directories of today and examples of blog search engines are Google's Blog search and Blog Search Engine.

The links created by blog directory submission are quite valuable and paid services can be used to enhance the amount of back links. Submission of blogs with high page ranking websites will help websites in gaining good rank. High page ranking websites are preferred by search engines and article directories function as a web traffic accelerator. Squidoo, HubPages and leading article submission websites are free sources of link creation. Anyone with a minimal knowledge of PHP can program WordPress themes and WordPress is one of the most business friendly web tools.

WordPress links seamlessly to MySQL database and building shopping cart is very simple with WordPress. WordPress for ecommerce allows securing website with a SSL certificate, password protect data, and monitoring transactions. The CMS of WordPress is designed keeping in mind the SEO and WordPress is a great boon for business. WordPress can be used to create powerful document management system and it comes with easy solutions to create forms. Selecting the services of freelance WordPress designer is a cost effective option and WordPress has over 18000 database plug-ins. User friendly layout of WordPress is beneficial for search engine optimization and integrating plug-ins with WordPress is essential for SEO benefits.

Image optimization is a key factor in improving search engine optimization results and a plug-in named as Smush.it is designed to delete excess image bytes from files. XML plug-in is an essential tool in a WordPress blog and working with a professional WordPress firm will help us to handle large and complex projects. WordPress development is used in forum portal, web directories, coupon sites and blogging sites. Interactivity, accessibility, usability and functionality are the coveted features of WordPress. The exclusive services offered by WordPress developers include WordPress design implementation, WordPress customized development, custom modules development and WordPress theme development.

Well known WordPress development companies offer the services of WordPress module installation, WordPress template development, and WordPress CMS Development. WordPress CMS allows modifying fonts, banners, graphics, logos, and widgets with great ease. Bloggers using a self hosted WordPress site won't have to worry about restrictions and it gives internet marketers the ability to learn more. FTP access to the site is another major feature of WordPress self hosted site and WordPress has become an excellent choice for personal blogs. Premium WordPress themes are elegant designs loaded with best elements of graphics and the list of most essential plug-ins in WordPress include that of SEO, backup, and antispam.

Website Vs Blog

Many internet users get confused about websites and blogs and they used to ask the question, "what is the difference between website and blog?" Website is a collection of interlinked web pages and blog is a website which uses content management system. A website often works as an official channel and a blog is often like an online diary. Creating blogs is very cheap when compared to creating websites and we could have a self hosted WordPress blog with $20. Blogs are cheap to maintain and they are easy to update and blogs allow written text, audio, as well as video.

The content in a website will be static whereas the content in a blog will be regularly updated. A website will be formal or professional where as the blog is completely informal. One way communication takes place in website and blogs feature great amount of interactivity. Website is the perfect platform to promote a product or website and a blog constantly supplies potential customers useful content. Blogs let us to develop and strengthen relationships and fresh as well as original content is an essential requirement for blogs. Many blogs have lots of useful features that promote interactivity and the objective of a blog is to provide helpful content.

Blogs are equipped with simple interface and all blogs are managed using a Content Management System. Creating a blog is the fastest and easiest way to get started online and blogs get more attention from search engines since they are dynamic. Blogs ping search engines every time new content is posted and most blogs allow readers to comment, discuss and participate. WordPress themes allow configuring blog as static website and the blogging component can be added as a separate section. Blogs feature a plug and play website model and the difference between blog and website is the difference in how the data is being presented.

A blog is basically a web log that uses chronological listing of blog posts and blogs thrive on new content. Basic features of blogs are commenting section, Really Simple Syndication (RSS) feeds, and archives section. A website is anything on the internet presented in HTML, CSS, JavaScript, Python and PHP. Website can be complimented with a blog and a website could be anything from a single page to one billion user social network. A typical website is characterized by home page, portfolio of work, frequently asked questions page, client testimonials, contact form and products/services page. If a person is concerned with creating content on a regular basis, he can select blog instead of website.

Websites represent a full featured online portal and website combined with blog is recommended for companies.

All blogs are websites

All websites are not blogs

Websites work as a virtual store that sells products or services and website is the perfect platform to self advertise. Blog software has the capability of providing us with both static pages (pages) and blog pages (posts). Both website and blog are necessary for the success of online exposure and the ease of developing the web presence is the number one attraction of websites.

Blogs and websites function well together and website features basic information whereas blogs feature extensive information. Websites feature inbound marketing while blogs feature both inbound and outbound marketing. Blogs are equipped with massive SEO whereas websites are powered with limited SEO only. Websites need easy navigation, splash pages, categorization and internal search. It has been pointed out that blogs are spontaneous in nature and they are great content marketing tools. Blog content often generates traffic, likes, links, as well as social shares and the definition of blog has changed as time passed by. Blogs are purely used for journal type entries and they allow us to publish content such as text, audio, video and images.

Optimizing the site for search engines is very easy with a blog and blogs are cheaper to build than static websites. Blogs of today function as powerful publishing platforms and it is the hub of all social media marketing. Social media sites are great for micro blogging and WordPress can be used to make a static or traditional website. The answer to the question, "should I start with a blog or website?" depends on the requirement. Websites will have more evergreen information and blog can be effectively used to write, publicize, promote and advertise content online.

The homepage of a website consists of things to browse and navigate internal website pages. Website content usually revolves around the same topic and blogs are more informative and educational. Blogs allow two way communication while websites allow only one way communication. The web pages in websites are not ordered by date and websites are equipped with self contained blog. The plus point of WordPress is that it can create blog, website, or website with blog. Blogs will have routine entries of commentaries, personal diaries, political opinions and videos. Blogging platform is a service that lets us to publish content in the form of a blog straight to the internet.

Websites can be versatile and they fill numerous purposes among others and a blog is weblog of some sort. Blogs are used by niche bloggers to share information about a particular segment and modern day blogs are called as digital magazines. Hybrid site is a traditional site which includes blog on the site and the blog can be used to support the traditional website. Static website is an online location which includes a landing page that doesn't change with time. The landing page on a blog contains the most up to date post available from the business owner.

According to seasoned website developers, it is easy and quick to develop a static website when compared with a blog. Websites are commonly used to sell products, provide after sales support and provide valuable information. Blog serves as an informal media for sharing news, information, views, and ideas about a particular topic. The proliferation of blogs can be attributed to the ease of creating a blog site and website offers great amount of flexibility. A blog could be as simple as diary of travel and interaction is the lifeblood of any blog of contemporary age. A person using blogs won't have to depend on another technical folk to make updates to his blog.

THANK YOU!

If you enjoyed this book or benefitted from it anyway, then I would like to ask you for a favour: would you be kind enough to leave a review for this book on Amazon.com? It would be greatly appreciated.

Click here to leave a review for this book on Amazon.com

Other Books by MAHINROOP PM

Mega Book of Website Designing